CONTENTS

- ASH AND PIKACHU 4
- BROCK 5
- DAWN 6
- TEAM ROCKET 7
- LOST LEADER STRATEGY 8
- POKÉDEX PROFILES 22
- CROSSING BATTLE LINES 28
- VEILSTONE VALUES 42
- BIRDS OF PREY COPY GRID 43
- MAYLENE'S MAZE 44
- FIRE AND ICE WORDSEARCH 45
- GIRATINA AND SHAYMIN 46
- PICK A POKÉDEX 48
- SINNOH SHUFFLE 49
- ANSWERS 50

POKÉ-FRIENDS FOREVER

ASH AND PIKACHU

Ash is a force to be reckoned with. Aged just ten he showed maturity and courage beyond his years when he took the decision to leave his home in Pallet Town and begin his long journey towards becoming a Pokémon Master. Dedicated and determined in his quest, he has overcome countless obstacles along the way – not least finding himself coupled from the outset with the most reluctant of Pokémon.

It's hard to believe Pikachu and Ash were ever anything other than firm friends, but initially the feisty electric Pokémon and the novice trainer didn't hit it off! Pikachu wouldn't listen to Ash's orders until Ash proved that he'd lay down his life for his pal. Ash's awesome gesture came when he defended Pikachu against threats from the evil Team Rocket and attacks from wild Pokémon.

Now their close bond and shared adventures mean that Ash and Pikachu can take on and beat even the most formidable of foes. The pair are more than ready to face the challenges which no doubt await them in Sinnoh. It's a vast land with treacherous terrain including a huge mountainous ridge, dense forests and towering cities. The coastal waters around Sinnoh are also teeming with Pokémon, each waiting to be discovered. Just who or what will the pair meet next?

POKÉ-FRIENDS FOREVER

BROCK

Brock is Ash's oldest friend and a true mastermind when it comes to Pokémon. His years as Pewter City Gym Leader mean that he has built up a huge knowledge of Pokémon skills and tactics! Luckily Brock's always happy to share his wisdom with his friends Ash and Dawn.

As well as being a revered breeder, Brock is thoughtful and creative. He loves to cook and is always quick to rustle up a bowl of his special food whenever he needs to re-energise a Pokémon exhausted from battle. It is in Sinnoh that Brock forms one of his closest Pokémon friendships, bonding with a Croagunk.

Brock's one weakness is a pretty face. Luckily whenever he gets misty-eyed over a girl, his friends are on hand to see he doesn't lose every shred of dignity. If all else fails Croagunk prods him back to reality with those painfully toxic fingers. Ouch!

POKÉ-FRIENDS FOREVER

DAWN

Ash and Brock liked Dawn from the moment they met her in Twin Leaf Town. Bursting with smiles and wisecracks – she can more than hold her own in their company! During their travels, Dawn has also proved herself to be a talented Pokémon Co-ordinator.

At times the young trainee is prone to dips in confidence when she loses a contest. In Sinnoh she'll have to take steps to combat the niggling self-doubt which has been creeping up on her following her last defeat. Deep down though, Dawn knows that she has what it takes to be the best.

Dawn's love of fashion means that she's ideally suited to the contests she takes part in. Pokémon entered in these competitions are judged on the beauty of their moves, rather than their ferocity in battle. Dawn even designed her Buneary's vest, although she admitted her mother was the one to sew it!

POKÉ-FRIENDS FOREVER

TEAM ROCKET

Jessie, James and Meowth form Team Rocket, a discontented band that travel from calamity to crisis in a hot air balloon. They live by the motto "a rose by any other name would smell as sweet, when everything's worse our work is complete". The trio would do anything to make trouble for our heroes.

Team Rocket is bad news – if Jessie, James and Meowth had more than one brain-cell between them they'd be dangerous! Luckily they're as stupid as they are wicked. So far all their plans have been scuppered, usually by arrogance and lack of planning.

Unfortunately the gang doesn't work alone. Mysterious and elusive boss Giovanni has ordered them to capture Ash's Pikachu because of its unique powers. Jessie, James and Meowth desperately want to impress their evil master, so they'll keep lying, cheating and stealing to achieve their goal.

PUT THE STICKERS DOWN IN THE RIGHT PLACES TO BRING THIS AWESOME NEW STORY TO LIFE!

ARRIVING IN VEILSTONE CITY, OUR HEROES UNEXPECTEDLY COME ACROSS NEW BATTLE CHALLENGES. CAN DAWN FACE HER OWN FEARS TO HELP ANOTHER AND WILL ASH MASTER AN INCREDIBLE NEW BATTLE MOVE?

LOST LEADER STRATEGY!

The attack continued, but the girl deftly repelled one after another of Lucario's moves. "Check out how she's deflecting those Aura Spheres!" said Ash.
The girl was desperately trying to defend herself.
"Lucario, you're angry at me, aren't you?" she cried, her voice wobbling.
"Are you using Bone Rush?" Ash and the gang watched as the girl fended off another power move.
"Lucario's acting awfully intense for a training session," said Dawn.

Ash, Brock and Dawn were heading for the Veilstone City Gym when the air around them suddenly began to shake.

"What in the world was that?" stammered Dawn.
"Aura Spheres," said Ash, as the group ran for cover.
"Look!" yelled Dawn as one sphere blasted a hole in the fence to reveal an athletic-looking girl with a bandaged nose and arm, fleeing a fearsome Pokémon.
"Lucario!" said Ash, pulling out his Pokédex just to make sure.

LUCARIO
THE AURA POKÉMON, AND THE EVOLVED FORM OF RIOLU. BY SENSING THE AURA OF ITS OPPONENTS, LUCARIO CAN READ THEIR THOUGHTS AND MOVEMENTS.

you're sorry."
The Pokémon stayed silent.
Before another row could erupt, a voice called "Maylene! What's happened?"
"Hi Reggie," replied Maylene.
A young man walked up, looking confused.
"Where exactly are you going Electabuzz?" asked Reggie, catching the Pokémon as it tried to slip away.
"Hey Pikachu," said Ash thoughtfully.

"Don't'cha think that looks like Paul's Electabuzz?" "That must mean you know Paul," said Reggie. "Is this the Pikachu that can use Volt Tackle? No wonder Electabuzz was giving you grief!"
The man smiled.
"I'm Paul's older brother," he went on. "I'm a Breeder, so Paul decided to leave all of his Pokémon here with me for a little training."

Before Brock or Ash had time to reply a bolt of electricity flew out from behind a nearby tree, knocking Piplup to the floor.

"Electabuzz!" yelled Ash as the striped, electric Pokémon emerged from its hiding place.
Piplup ran towards it followed by Pikachu. Before long they were immersed in an ugly brawl.
"Cut it out," shouted Brock.
"Knock it off!" bellowed Ash.
"We've got to help Lucario," said the girl, pointing at the clashing Pokémon. Lucario sent an Aura Sphere with such force it knocked Piplup and Pikachu into a heap.
"I'm so sorry!" said the girl. "Lucario, say

Ash introduced himself. "My name is Ash and I came here to challenge the Veilstone Gym!" he grinned. "Has Paul had a battle there yet?"

"Yeah, he defeated her," replied Reggie, pointing at Maylene. The girl stared at the floor in embarrassment.
"Whoa!" gasped Ash. "She's the Gym Leader?"
He felt surprised and thrilled to have accidentally stumbled on the exact person he was looking for.
"Can we have a Gym Battle soon?" he asked, not predicting Maylene's answer…

"Sorry, but would you mind going to some other gym instead," Maylene murmured meekly, only to be sent flying by Lucario again.
Reggie stepped forward to explain. "Lucario's not happy with Maylene as a battle partner yet."
"What about all those Aura Spheres we saw?" asked Dawn.
"That must've been Lucario training the Trainer!" said an amazed Brock.

From their vantage point behind a nearby bush, Team Rocket were well within earshot of the conversation. In fact, they had spied the whole sorry episode.

"So Lucario rules," smirked James. "While that Gym Leader drools," chuckled Jessie.
An evil plan began to form in Meowth's tiny mind. "If we could draft that dynamo then we'd stop drooling and some of that ruling might just rub off on us!"
With Lucario on their side, Team Rocket couldn't fail to succeed in capturing Pikachu!

Unaware of this plotting, Maylene picked herself up after Lucario's latest onslaught.
"I told you to STOP!" she yelled.
"Unacceptable," replied a stern voice.
Three men in martial arts gear approached – according to Reggie they were students at the Gym, eager to toughen up Maylene. It seemed that the men respected the girl as a battler but not a leader.
"I thought I might find you here," said the biggest, a black belt called Connally.
"I'm not going back to the Gym!" announced Maylene. "I don't want to be Gym Leader anymore."

"**I**s it because of Paul?" asked Reggie. He described to Ash, Brock and Dawn how Paul had defeated Maylene by using flying Pokémon in her Fighting-type Gym.

"It didn't even look like a battle," admitted Maylene. "And I can hardly blame the challenger for what he said to me."

"What did he say?" asked Ash. Maylene winced at the memory. "You're the weakest Gym Leader I ever fought, and this lightweight badge is just like you."
Suddenly she ran off, shouting behind her. "He was right!"
"I'm sorry," said Reggie. "You've travelled a long way."
"Let's find another gym with a more battle-willing leader," suggested Brock.

Just as the gang were preparing to leave, Dawn asked to speak with Maylene. When Reggie nodded his agreement, Lucario accompanied Dawn to a secluded spot where they found the forlorn girl.
As soon as they had gone, Reggie turned to Brock and Ash, then shrugged. "Maylene simply doesn't believe in herself anymore."

"I know just how you feel," Dawn said gently, sitting beside her new friend. "I didn't get past round one for two contests in a row."

Maylene put her head in her hands. Suddenly Dawn dropped a bombshell. "I'm taking a break. I tell everyone I'm just recharging my batteries, but to be honest sometimes I think I'm not cut out for contests!"

"I can't concentrate like I used to," muttered Maylene. "After Reggie's brother said those things about me I just can't go on being a Gym Leader." But the girls' heart-to-heart was due to be cut short.

"Relax! Your troubles are history!" yelled Jessie, jumping out with James and Meowth. "Are these friends of yours?" Maylene asked.

"We're here to offer lucky Lucario a better deal," smirked Jessie.
"A winning warrior like Lucario deserves to side with someone stronger than this Gym Leader Loser!" added James.
The mean trio started to bribe Lucario with promises of rides in their airship and bars of chocolate until the Pokémon sent them flying with a single blow.
"Maybe he was allergic to chocolate?" screeched Jessie.
"I think he was allergic to *you*!" yelped Meowth.
The hapless threesome were blasting off once again.

Maylene thanked Dawn. "I bet you're still mad at me though," she said to Lucario.

Eager to boost Maylene's spirits, Dawn told the worried Gym Leader that Lucario's anger was only because he really cared for her.

"I know!" clapped Dawn. "Let's you and I battle."
Maylene looked at Lucario. He could hardly contain his delight.
"You're on!" she grinned.
Back in the house, Reggie was feeding Pikachu and Chimchar while he and Ash were arranging their own battle.
"I know it's no substitute for the

Veilstone Gym," said Reggie. "But I'd really like to see how Paul's rival stacks up."
As they boys headed outside they passed an impressive medal cabinet.
"Are these all Paul's?" asked Brock in awe.
"No Brock," Reggie answered.
"They're mine."

The girls returned just in time to see Reggie and Ash square up.

Ash summoned his first Pokémon.
"Turtwig I choose you!"
Reggie chose Bibarel and the battle began.
"Turtwig, Energy Ball. Let's go!"

"Bibarel," commanded Reggie. "Use Super Fang!"
The Pokémon's moves cancelled each other out, but thanks to Bibarel's Secret Power Turtwig was soon on the floor.
"Secret Power's effect changes depending on the field," explained Brock. "This is a grassy area, so it put Turtwig to sleep!"

"Now use Take Down," ordered Reggie. Bibarel's move threw the sleeping Turtwig up in the air. To everyone's surprise the crash landing woke him up. Reggie tried Super Fang.
"Dodge it! Then Razor Leaf," countered Ash.
"I like the way your Turtwig moves," said Reggie, impressed.
"Thanks Reggie, that move came from watching Gardenia and her Turtwig at the Eterna Gym!" said Ash, ordering Energy Ball again.
Reggie used Bibarel's Ice Beam, but Turtwig finished Bibarel off with one more Energy Ball.
"Nice going Turtwig," cheered Ash. "One for us!"

15

"Isn't that something?" squealed Dawn. "Ash and Turtwig have been practising really hard."

"That's wonderful," beamed Maylene. It was time for round two.
"Swalot! You're up next!" called Reggie. Ash brought Turtwig back in to fight then looked his new opponent up in his Pokédex.

SWALOT
THE POISON BAG POKÉMON, SPRAYS A POWERFUL POISON ONTO ITS OPPONENTS FROM ITS PORES.

Ash listened intently before making his decision. "OK Staravia, I choose you!" Staravia started well with Wing Attack, but Reggie just called "Stockpile." Swalot seemed to do nothing.
"Why don't they counter attack?" Dawn asked Brock.
Brock explained that while Swalot's flexible body was resisting damage, Stockpile enabled it to store up power at the same time. Sure enough, when Staravia came at Swalot using Aerial Ace Swalot spat out its power, sending Ash's Pokémon reeling.

As soon as Staravia had recovered, Ash tried Aerial Ace again.

Reggie ordered Swalot to retaliate with Sludgebomb, knocking Staravia from the sky.
A win for Reggie took the score to one all but as ever, win or lose, Ash was quick to thank his Pokémon for its efforts.
"Staravia! You were awesome," he said as the bird flew down to his shoulder and then back into the Poké Ball.
"I'm completely impressed with your Staravia's amazing skills!" said Reggie. "But there's a move I'd love to show you."
"That'd be great!" replied Ash happily.
"I bet I know who's coming next," said Maylene from the sidelines.
"The evolved form of Staravia," gasped Ash in amazement as Reggie summoned Staraptor from his Poké Ball. Ash listened intently to the Pokédex description of the breathtaking creature.

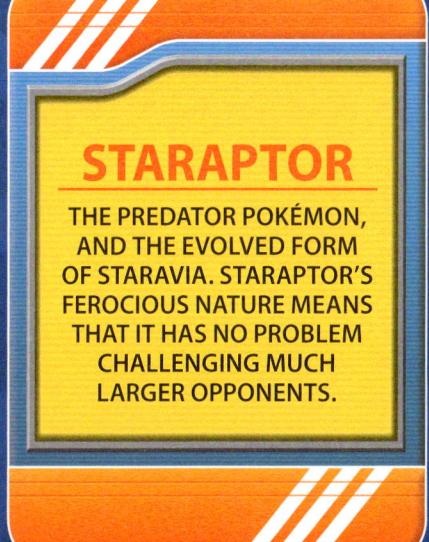

STARAPTOR

THE PREDATOR POKÉMON, AND THE EVOLVED FORM OF STARAVIA. STARAPTOR'S FEROCIOUS NATURE MEANS THAT IT HAS NO PROBLEM CHALLENGING MUCH LARGER OPPONENTS.

"**Staravia watch closely, OK.**" The young Trainer thought for a moment, then called on his most trusted Pokémon friend.

"Pikachu, Get in there," said Ash, urging Pikachu into battle
"All right, bring it on Ash!" called Reggie feverishly, watching as Staraptor climbed overhead.
Pikachu hopped up and down waiting for Ash's next instruction.
As soon as the Trainer cried "Okay Pikachu, Thunderbolt!" the usual crackle of electricity erupted from Pikachu's tail.
Reggie countered with his power move Brave Bird, transforming Staraptor into a plummeting ball of flame.
Pikachu spun on Ash's command, but was no match for this incredible move. The electric Pokémon was hurled to the floor, where he lay stunned and seemingly lifeless.

"Pikachu!" shouted Ash in alarm, as the moments ticked past.
Slowly the resilient little Pokémon began to stir. He was going to be OK.

"**I**'m surprised your Pikachu's up so quick!" said Reggie. Ash smiled, but looked very relieved.

On the sidelines Dawn was equally shocked by what she'd just witnessed. "Did Staraptor take damage too?" she asked Brock, sure the Breeder would have the answer.

Brock nodded. "Brave Bird's a risky move because it can cause damage to the one using it in the first place."

"You have to have a lot of confidence in your speed and power!" Maylene piped up.

Until that point she had remained totally silent, but her excited tone and twinkling eyes showed that she'd loved every second of the battle so far. Was this the turning point for Veilstone's new Gym Leader?

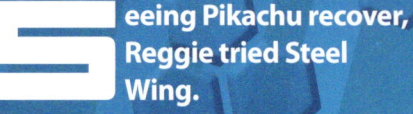

Seeing Pikachu recover, Reggie tried Steel Wing.

"Iron Tail!" cried Ash.
"Pikachu's incredible!" whispered Maylene. "To say nothing of Ash." Witnessing Staraptor duck Iron Tail, Ash sent Pikachu back in using Volt Tail. "Staraptor, use Wing Attack to counter!" Reggie yelled into the air at the top of his voice.
The plucky Pokémon clashed in a ball of energy. At first it seemed that Pikachu had come off worse, but he opened his eyes just in time to watch Staraptor drop to the ground like a stone.
The gang erupted in cheers while the other battle stars Chimchar, Gligar and Staravia made their delight known too. "That's two out of three, so Ash Wins!" cried Brock proudly.

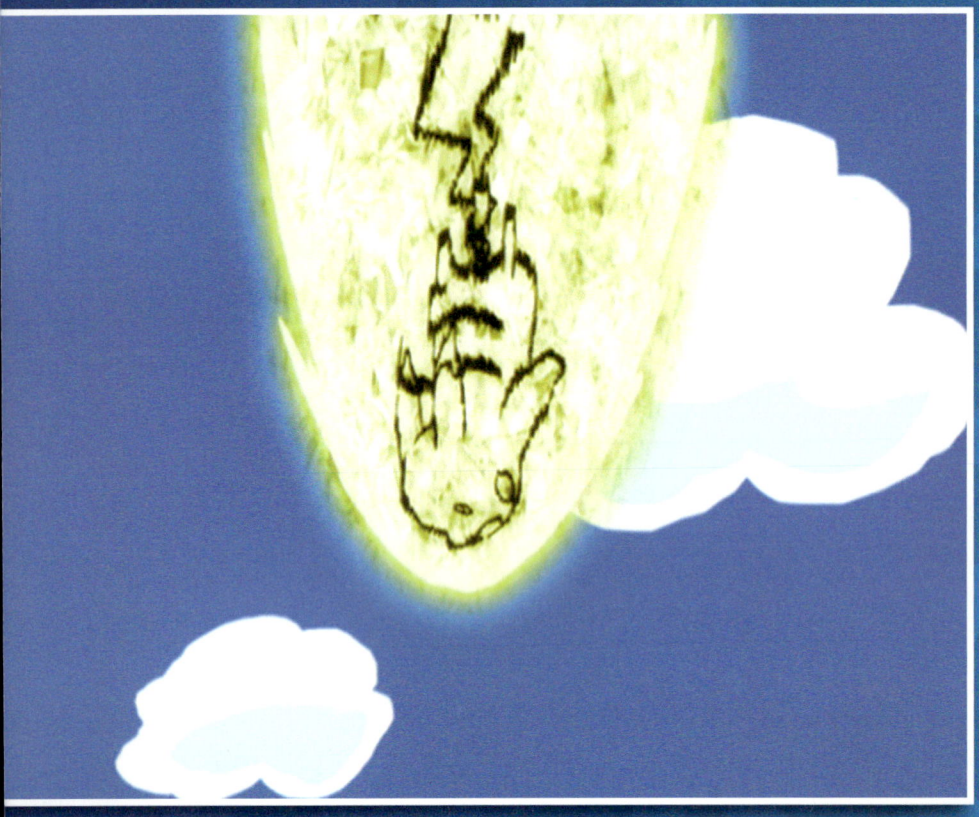

"**R**eggie, thanks for everything," said Ash.

"I can't remember the last time I had such a great battle!" replied Reggie. "And now if you still want, I'd like to show you that move."

"I'll bet it's Brave Bird," guessed Ash. Reggie nodded. "Staravia will pick it up in a flash."

But there was one final surprise in store for Ash. Reggie asked Maylene if she'd now consider battling him. "Excuse me," said Dawn firmly. "I asked Maylene first!"

It appears Veilstone City is full of surprises as Dawn announces her unexpected Gym Battle debut. Will she have the courage to see it through and will Maylene take up her challenge?

TO BE CONTINUED...

POKÉDEX PROFILES

LUCARIO

TYPE:	FIGHTING-STEEL
ABILITY:	STEADFAST/INNER FOCUS
HEIGHT:	1.2m
WEIGHT:	54kg

Evolved from Riolu, Lucario has the amazing ability to sense and read the auras of all things and therefore predict their thoughts and movements. It also understands human speech.

STORY SECRET: When battling Piplup, Lucario used new and devastating move Palm Force to win the day.

MEDITITE

TYPE:	FIGHTING-PSYCHIC
ABILITY:	PURE POWER
HEIGHT:	0.6m
WEIGHT:	11.2kg

This curious blue creature eats just one berry a day. By enduring hunger Meditite's spirit gets sharpened. It evolves into Medicham.

PIPLUP

TYPE:	WATER
ABILITY:	TORRENT
HEIGHT:	0.4m
WEIGHT:	5.2kg

The penguin-like Pokémon favoured by Dawn is a skilled swimmer and diver. Piplup prefers to dwell and hunt on the shores of the northern lakes. It evolves into Prinplup and the powerful Empoleon.

STORY SECRET: When Piplup fought Lucario, it used a powerful combination of Whirlpool and Peck.

POKÉDEX PROFILES

STARAPTOR

TYPE:	NORMAL-FLYING
ABILITY:	INTIMIDATE
HEIGHT:	1.2m
WEIGHT:	24.9kg

Having evolved from Staravia, this formidable Pokémon is certainly not to be messed with. The bird-like creature will courageously challenge foes that are much larger than itself.

AMBIPOM

TYPE:	NORMAL
ABILITY:	TECHNICIAN/PICKUP
HEIGHT:	1.2m
WEIGHT:	20.3kg

Unlike its first evolution Aipom, Ambipom rarely uses its arms at all anymore. It performs even the trickiest tasks with its two tails. These are also used for linking – as a sign of friendship.

STORY SECRET: In combat Dawn chooses Ambipom, because of all the battle experience he has gained with Ash.

MURKROW

TYPE:	DARK-FLYING
ABILITY:	INSOMNIA/SUPER LUCK
HEIGHT:	0.5m
WEIGHT:	2.1kg

Rather like black cats and humans, it is believed that seeing this Pokémon at night brings the witness bad luck. Murkrow evolves into Honchkrow.

POKÉDEX PROFILES

STARAVIA

TYPE:	NORMAL-FLYING
ABILITY:	INTIMIDATE
HEIGHT:	0.6m
WEIGHT:	15.5kg

In the wild this Pokémon sticks within a huge flock for protection. It flies around forests and fields in search of bug Pokémon. Staravia evolves from tiny Starly.

STORY SECRET: At first Staravia has trouble picking up Staraptor's amazing power move Brave Bird, but it is conquered in the end.

HONCHCROW

TYPE:	DARK-FLYING
ABILITY:	INSOMNIA/SUPER LUCK
HEIGHT:	0.9m
WEIGHT:	27.3kg

After it has evolved this nocturnal Pokémon becomes almost ten times its previous weight. It soon treats other Murkrow like servants, ordering them to bring it food. It swarms with numerous Murkrow in tow.

BUNEARY

TYPE:	NORMAL
ABILITY:	RUN AWAY/KLUTZ
HEIGHT:	0.4m
WEIGHT:	5.5kg

This cute and harmless looking Pokémon whips foes by swiftly unfurling its coiled ears. It stings enough to make a grown-up weep in pain, but evolves into the cautious Lopunny.

STORY SECRET: Buneary literally bounces its way out of trouble when Meditite uses Drain Punch.

POKÉDEX PROFILES

ABOMASNOW

TYPE:	GRASS-ICE
ABILITY:	SNOW WARNING
HEIGHT:	2.2m
WEIGHT:	135.5kg

What we humans refer to as the mythical 'abominable snowman' or 'yeti' is actually this colossal Pokémon. It evolves from Snover, whipping up blizzards in mountains to ensure that they're always buried in snow.

DRIFLOON

TYPE:	GHOST-FLYING
ABILITY:	AFTERMATH/UNBURDEN
HEIGHT:	0.4m
WEIGHT:	1.2kg

This bizarre creature is formed by the spirits of Pokémon and people too. It loves damp, humid seasons. Drifloon mysteriously evolves into Drifblim.

HAPPINY

TYPE:	NORMAL
ABILITY:	NATURAL CURE/SERENE GRACE
HEIGHT:	0.6m
WEIGHT:	24.4kg

It loves white things, preferring to a waddle about with an egg-shaped rock. Happiny parades with an egg in imitation of its next evolution, Chansey.

STORY SECRET: Brock bonds well with Happiny, Often choosing to pet them on his lap and stroke them to sleep.

POKÉDEX PROFILES

PACHIRISU

TYPE:	ELECTRIC
ABILITY:	RUN AWAY/PICKUP
HEIGHT:	0.4m
WEIGHT:	3.9kg

Its cute squirrel-like exterior hides a dangerous and tough opponent. Pachirisu makes fur balls which crackle with static electricity. In the wild it stores them in tree holes.

SPIRITOMB

TYPE:	GHOST-DARK
ABILITY:	PRESSURE
HEIGHT:	1.0m
WEIGHT:	108kg

This strange-looking Pokémon doesn't evolve. It was somehow formed by 108 spirits. Spiritomb is attached to a crack in a keystone.

TURTWIG

TYPE:	GRASS
ABILITY:	OVERGROW
HEIGHT:	0.4m
WEIGHT:	10.2kg

Turtwig makes oxygen with its body through photosynthesis. The leaf on its head wilts and its shell softens if it gets thirsty. The Grass Pokémon evolves to Grotle and then Torterra.

STORY SECRET: Turtwig's use of Energy Ball wins the day when he battles Maylene's Bibarel.

POKÉDEX PROFILES

GABITE

TYPE:	DRAGON-GROUND
ABILITY:	SAND VEIL
HEIGHT:	1.4m
WEIGHT:	56kg

Gabite is the middle evolution between Gible and Garchomp. It is worth looking out for as there is a long-held belief that medicine made from its scales will heal even incurable illnesses.

HIPPOPOTAS

TYPE:	GROUND
ABILITY:	SAND STREAM
HEIGHT:	0.8m
WEIGHT:	49.5kg

It lives in dry places because it hates to get wet. Instead of perspiration, Hippopotas sweats out grainy sand from its body. It evolves into Hippowdon.

CHIMCHAR

TYPE:	FIRE
ABILITY:	BLAZE
HEIGHT:	0.5m
WEIGHT:	6.2kg

A great climber, it lives on mountain tops, transforming into Monferno then Infernape. Nothing can extinguish its fire, although the flame automatically goes out when Chimchar sleeps.

THE ADVENTURE CONTINUES! THIS COOL STORY HAS GOT MORE SPACE FOR YOUR FIERCEST POKÉMON STICKERS.

CROSSING BATTLE LINES

THE TIME FOR DAWN'S CHALLENGE TO MAYLENE, THE VEILSTONE GYM LEADER, IS FINALLY HERE. OUR TALENTED YOUNG CO-ORDINATOR IS READY TO LEAVE HER CONTEST COMFORT ZONE TO TRY HER HAND AT BATTLING, BUT IS VICTORY REALLY HER GOAL?

Battle day was fast approaching. Dawn stood by the stream, putting her Pokémon through their paces.

"Keep an eye on how Buizel moves!" she told Piplup as it tried to copy Buizel's rhythmic punches. "Have you decided which Pokémon you're going to use?" asked Brock.
"Maylene's using Fighting types, so I've decided to start with Piplup since it can use a Flying-type move," announced Dawn. "Next I'll take advantage of all the battle experience Ambipom got with Ash, then I'll use Buneary with its awesome jumping skills!"
"Sounds good to me," said Brock, watching Dawn's team of Pokémon working hard.

"Staravia, Brave Bird, now," Ash ordered. Staravia began well, but wobbled. Its power disappeared like a light bulb switching off and it crash-landed. "Looks like Staravia lost its balance at the moment of power release," Reggie offered. "Now, maybe if we were to use a moving target instead of a rock we could work on improving Staravia's concentration…"
Reggie couldn't believe his ears when Ash courageously offered to be the target himself. "Anything to make Staravia stronger," Ash explained.

In another part of the field Reggie was showing Ash how to use Brave Bird.

The pair called Staraptor and Staravia from their Poké Balls. As the flying Pokémon soared overhead, Reggie gave Staraptor the command to transform into a ball of flaming energy. They both watched as Staraptor zapped and destroyed a nearby rock. "Man, what power," gasped Ash. Soon it was his turn to try.
"Scared Ash?" asked Reggie.
"No way!" came the reply.

 **rock strolled over. "Typical training for Ash," he chuckled.**

"I kind of feel like I should stop him," said Reggie before enquiring about Dawn's progress.
"She's ready to go, all right," said Brock. "But why would a Co-ordinator fight a Gym Battle?" Reggie asked.
"I honestly think Dawn's going through this just to help Maylene get her confidence back," Brock explained. "Dawn knows Maylene's a little shaky right now, and she really wants her to rediscover her love of battling."
Inside, Maylene and Lucario were meditating.

"I'm going to take this challenge very seriously," the Gym Leader told her companion, before asking a proud and excited Connally to referee.
Spying through a window, Team Rocket watched Lucario closely.
"Let's grab it," whispered Meowth. Jessie wasn't about to make the mistake of taking on the formidable Lucario again. "Since every time we try to poach primo Pokémon we fail miserably, I suggest Plan B! We grab a weaker Pokémon and train to our sneaky hearts' content!"
Jessie smirked at her own cleverness. "Then Plan B becomes Plan A!" James and Meowth were speechless.

That night Ash, Brock and Dawn stood on the balcony in the moonlight, talking about the day to come.

"This is my first Gym Battle and I have to admit I've got a case of nerves!" Dawn said.

"Every time I battle I get sweaty and my heart starts pounding and it feels like there's a train going through my head!" grinned Ash, adding that he hoped the battle would help Maylene stop doubting herself.

"I used to feel exactly the same way back at the Pewter Gym," Brock piped up from his armchair. The Breeder had been stroking a sleepy Happiny. "When I first started I was worried about what I was doing, but after meeting lots of trainers I learned that great Gym Leaders are shaped by their challengers!"

"So Dawn's battle could really help Maylene go up a level," said Ash excitedly.

"That's it!" said Brock. "It's going to be great!"

The next morning dawned bright and early.

On the roof of a building opposite the Gym, Team Rocket were barely visible behind the mountain of technology they were using to detect Pokémon suitable for capture.

"I've got cameras cranking all over that Gym!" said James.

Suddenly he spotted Dawn, Ash and Brock heading for the entrance.

"Don't those punks have enough Pokémon?" moaned Meowth.

"Twerps don't thieve, they're here to battle," replied James.

Inside the Gym the mood was equally tense. Connally explained the three-on-three rules. Only Dawn could substitute Pokémon and the battle would be over when all three Pokémon on one side could no longer fight.

mmediately Maylene called forth Meditite. Dawn had her Pokédex at the ready.

MEDITITE

THE MEDITATE POKÉMON. MEDITITE USES MEDITATIONS TO INCREASE ITS POWER, NEVER SKIPPING A SINGLE DAY OF YOGA.

"Now it's Dawn's turn!" whispered Ash excitedly.
Dawn seemed to have frozen.
"Uh oh," gulped Reggie. "Looks like Dawn's getting nervous!"
Luckily, Ash's knack for instilling confidence came to the fore.
"Dawn, have fun out there!" he yelled.
"Maylene! You're a Gym Leader remember, so show your strength!" It worked.
Maylene positively glowed with delight at Ash's words. Dawn snapped out of her crisis, calling for Buneary.
"Let the battle begin," said Connally. Quick as a flash, Dawn ordered Buneary to use Bounce.
Maylene however shouted for Detect, enabling Meditite to predict and dodge Buneary's next moves.
"Drain Punch, now!" shouted Maylene. Brock and Ash looked on in awe as Maylene and Meditite moved in perfect sync.
"Since she's a warrior Maylene mirrors her Pokémon's moves, making her even stronger!" said Reggie proudly as Meditite's Drain Punch floored Buneary. Outside, Team Rocket were having second thoughts about capturing the impressive Meditite.
"I think we're better off with Plan C," gulped Jessie.

The instant Buneary recovered, Dawn sent him straight back at Meditite with Ice Beam, trapping Meditite in a frozen block.

Dawn's tactic seemed to be working until Maylene called "Confusion!" Suddenly Meditite broke through the ice, sending it flying towards Buneary.

The Pokémon had to leap frantically from side-to-side to avoid injury from the jagged slivers.
"Confusion!" cried Maylene again. Before Dawn could react Buneary was being pulled into the air by an invisible force and then smashed back down.
"Bounce!" yelled Dawn.
Somehow Buneary managed to block the impact, landing on its feet beside Dawn.
"Way to go!" cheered Ash in support. The Gym Leader had one more move up her sleeve however.
"Drain Punch" she cried.
Again Buneary took the blow, but tried to bounce rather than fall. It just about landed but then its legs slowly gave way.
Maylene had won the first round.

"**T**hank you Buneary," said Dawn, assuring it that all its good work wouldn't go to waste. "Ambipom, you're next."

As Ash and Brock clapped, Dawn got to work.

"Swift, let's go!" she yelled. Ambipom shot out a tidal wave of stars, which surrounded and hit Meditite.
Maylene's Pokémon countered with Drain Punch. Somehow Ambipom managed to block the barrage of blows, using its amazing arms and huge hands.
"Double Hit," laughed Dawn.
"Wow!" exclaimed Reggie as Ambipom's arms rained down on Meditite, knocking it to the ground.
"Meditite is unable to battle," ruled Conally.
It was one round a-piece, but who would be the ultimate victor?

maylene was intrigued by Dawn's style and tactics. "It seems that you approach a battle like a contest."

"I guess so," Dawn replied. "I'm having a lot of fun doing it too!"
Suddenly the Gym Leader was no longer phased.
"Lucario, you ready to go?" she asked, before warning it not to be taken in by Dawn's contest-like moves.
On the sidelines, Ash and Brock noticed the difference in both the Leader and her Pokémon.

"The bond between those two is strong!" said Reggie. "Lucario must be sensing the confidence welling up inside Maylene."
Although Dawn had Ambipom use a confident Double Hit, Maylene pulled Bone Rush in perfect harmony with Lucario. It began thrusting and twirling its weapon while Ambipom tried to deflect the blows with its hands.
It was no use.
Ash gasped as Lucario caught Ambipom with a huge strike, sending it staggering to the floor. Dawn's Pokémon was KO'ed.

Ash was blown away. "Every movement with a purpose," gushed Brock.

"When Maylene and Lucario are working perfectly in sync – let's just say I defy anyone to find any kind of opening," chuckled Reggie. It certainly looked as if Dawn had reawakened Maylene's passion for battling.

Dawn however was not done yet! She gave herself a stiff talking to. "She's a Gym Leader all right with incredible strength! But…I'm not exactly a beginner either!"

With that, the young Co-ordinator called out Piplup, ordering it to use Bubble Beam.

"Dodge it, then use Aura Sphere," commanded Maylene.
The Sphere hit Piplup squarely, knocking him down and drawing gasps from the audience.

"That was a direct hit!" said a concerned Brock.
But Piplup wasn't finished yet. Opening one eye, it looked directly at Dawn.

"Use Whirlpool!" begged Dawn. The plucky penguin Pokémon whipped up a whirlpool within seconds, trapping the stunned Lucario in the centre.

"It's time to use Peck," shrieked Dawn, above the roar of gushing water. "Let's go!"
"Check it out!" said Ash. "Using contest techniques to cover their bad match-up," mused Reggie. "Nice strategy."

37

"**L**ucario, quick!" cried Maylene. "Metal Claw, right now!"

"Awesome move!" Dawn said with admiration.
"Hey, you too," smiled Maylene.

The girls were really having fun now. "They're both looking great!' said Ash happily.
"Maylene and Lucario are totally in sync," agreed Reggie. "And it has everything to do with Dawn's passionate battling style stirring things up!"
"Now, Piplup, Bubblebeam!" Dawn cried.
"Lucario, let's go," said Maylene, sending her Pokémon running into the direct line of Piplup's energy bubble jet stream. Lucario only stopped when he had Piplup balanced against his palm.
"What?" said Dawn, amazed that it had managed to reach Piplup at all.

"**F**orce Palm!" countered Maylene. A surge of power from Lucario's palm was followed by a blinding flash. Piplup was propelled up through the air and back down to the hard floor.

"What kind of move was that?" asked Ash.

"Force Palm is a Fighting-type move," explained Reggie. "First you get past your opponent's defence and then hit them with massive energy focused in your palm."

"Drat, stuck on the horns of a dilemma," said Jessie, as she watched Piplup go down. "Sounds like you're back to pursuing Plan A again," said James dryly. Jessie dismissed him angrily. "No duh! Lucario's primo."

"And if we try to poach him we'll get a primo pounding!" agreed Meowth.

Back in the Gym, Lucario and Piplup were still locked in battle.

"Lucario, use Aura Sphere!"
"Piplup, Peck!"
Dawn could see that the little blue Pokémon was looking tired.
"We can still win this thing," she urged.
Maylene had other ideas. "We'll break down their combinations Lucario!" Lucario threw another Aura Sphere, while Piplup reacted with Bubblebeam. Dawn's Pokémon frantically stored energy in order to deliver its most awesome Peck ever.

"Look out!" warned Dawn, but it was too late.
Lucario was on Piplup again with Force Palm! There was nowhere to hide. Piplup dropped to the floor, signalling an end to the fight.
As the exhausted, but happy girls thanked their Pokémon they had no idea that on a neighbouring roof their arch enemies were also throwing in the towel.
"Gobs of grunt work and we already knew Lucario was tops!" moaned James.
"All those cameras and not a trace of alternate Pokémon in sight!" sighed Jessie as the trio sloped sadly away.

"I don't know how to thank you Dawn," beamed Maylene. "I forgot all about my fears about winning or losing. All I could think was how much fun that was!"

"That means so much to me," said Dawn, clearly thrilled.
Brock put an arm around his friend. "Your strategy really paid off." Dawn smiled. "Yeah and soon Piplup and I'll be on the sidelines cheering for Ash, right?" "If that's the case I've got another fun battle to look forward to!" grinned Maylene. "And once my Staravia perfects that new move," laughed Ash. "You can be sure I'll be right back here to challenge you!"

Thanks to Dawn, the fiery spirit of a Gym Leader has once again been ignited within Maylene's soul. This promises to give Ash a challenge he'll never forget when he returns to fight at the Veilstone Gym in the future. We can't wait!

VEILSTONE VALUES

Now Maylene's re-discovered her love for Pokémon training and battling, she's back in business as Veilstone Gym Leader! The gym itself is once again a place of excellence, where great trainers like Ash can flourish.
Work your way through the grid, linking the words which describe the values Maylene insists upon from those who come to do battle in her gym.

RAGE		SURRENDER		DISRESPECT		ENVY
	CRUELTY		WICKEDNESS		DISOBEDIENCE	
DETERMINATION		BOREDOM		JEALOUSY		DISORDER
	COURAGE		IDLENESS		GREED	
IMPATIENCE		PASSION		LAZINESS		RUTHLESSNESS
	UNKINDNESS		DISCIPLINE		RESPECT	
MALICE		SPITE		INTELLIGENCE		PATIENCE
	CONFUSION		ANGER		RESENTMENT	
CHAOS		RUDENESS		SLYNESS		DEDICATION
	CHEATING		IGNORANCE		COWARDICE	

BIRDS OF PREY COPY GRID

GREAT BALLS OF FIRE! WHEN THEY ATTACK WITH THEIR RED-HOT BRAVE BIRD MOVE, STARAPTOR AND STARAVIA CAN BLAST ANY OPPONENT. ARE YOU READY TO TAKE THEM ON? IF SO, COPY THESE FANTASTIC PICTURES INTO THE EMPTY GRID, SQUARE-BY-SQUARE. NOW COLOUR THEM IN FOR MAXIMUM EFFECT.

43

MAYLENE'S MAZE

MAYLENE IS SUPPOSED TO BE TRAINING WITH LUCARIO TODAY BUT SHE CAN'T FIND THE WAY TO THEIR MEETING PLACE. HELP HER BY TRACING THE CORRECT ROUTE WITH A PEN OR PENCIL. HURRY BEFORE HE LOSES HIS TEMPER AND AN AURA SPHERE COMES FLYING YOUR WAY!

START

FINISH

FIRE & ICE WORDSEARCH

When these Pokémon mix it up, they make an awesome combination! Find the missing stickers for the Fire and Ice types below, then cross each name off the wordsearch grid. You'll have to study the letters carefully – the daring dozen could be hiding in any direction!

M	A	M	O	S	W	I	N	E	T	R	R
W	O	N	S	A	M	O	B	A	E	I	A
P	D	W	F	O	J	U	Q	V	U	S	P
M	O	N	F	E	R	N	O	F	E	M	I
W	H	A	R	N	C	N	T	H	P	L	D
E	L	P	O	K	S	L	C	X	A	W	A
A	G	D	S	V	E	B	P	E	N	F	S
V	K	W	L	S	G	S	O	J	R	L	H
I	G	L	A	C	E	O	N	B	E	H	K
L	V	E	S	Z	X	M	Y	D	F	G	Y
E	N	Y	S	J	E	R	T	Q	N	A	B
S	C	H	I	M	C	H	A	R	I	R	N

- ☐ MAMOSWINE
- ☐ SNOVER
- ☐ GLACEON
- ☐ SNEASEL
- ☐ INFERNAPE
- ☐ FROSLASS
- ☐ RAPIDASH
- ☐ WEAVILE
- ☐ MONFERNO

☐ CHIMCHAR

☐ ABOMASNOW

☐ PONYTA

45

46

MEET SHAYMIN AND GIRATINA

that threaten its home or food stores. Shaymin has a unique purity that enables it to breath in dirty fumes and exhale pristine, fresh air. It can also transform spoiled areas into oases of lush flowers.

Giratina is rarely sighted in Sinnoh. It is believed that the Ghost Dragon Pokémon dwells in its own mirror realm, known as Reverse World. Little is known about this parallel dimension, but it is said that here Giratina moves in its Origin Forme. In both states it is agreed that the creature is extremely powerful. It can be easily identified by its sharp gold claws and the red stripes running down its body.

Sinnoh storytellers say that once a Shaymin stumbled onto the path of an incensed Giratina. The Ghost Dragon Pokémon was locked in battle with Dialga, believing the ancient deity to have polluted its home. The intensity of the combat dragged the Shaymin into Giratina's Reverse World, provoking a catastrophic series of events that would draw Ash and his friends into the most challenging adventure of their lifetimes…

Shaymin is a tiny, wild Pokémon that nestles in dells of flowers. In its shy Land Forme it uses its petal-like ears and grassy fur to skillfully hide itself amongst the flora. When it grows anxious, Shaymin will curl itself up into a ball until danger has passed. The Grass Pokémon's Sky Forme is bolder however, taking on challengers

PICK A POKÉDEX

THERE ARE SOME INCREDIBLE POKÉMON TRAINING AT THE VEILSTONE GYM! ASH AND DAWN KNOW THAT REGGIE AND MAYLENE WILL PRESENT THEM WITH A SERIES OF TOUGH OPPONENTS. STUDY THE POKÉDEX SCREEN AT THE TOP AND THEN TICK THE SCREEN BELOW THAT MATCHES IT EXACTLY.

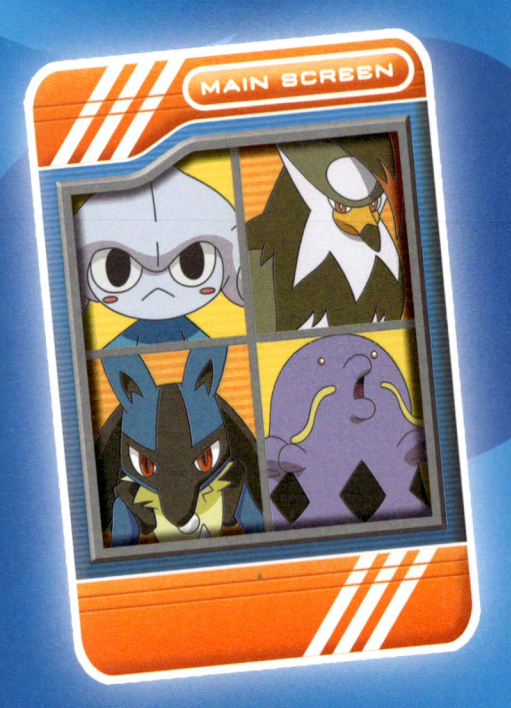

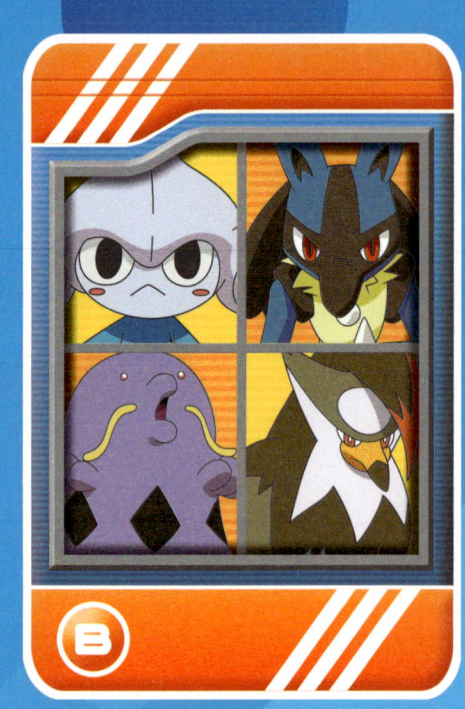

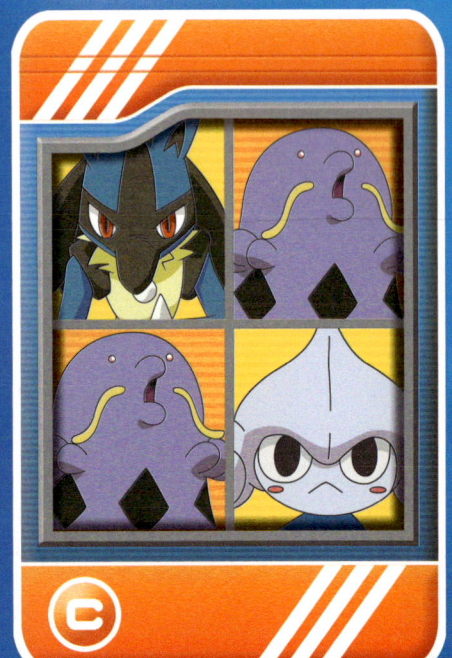

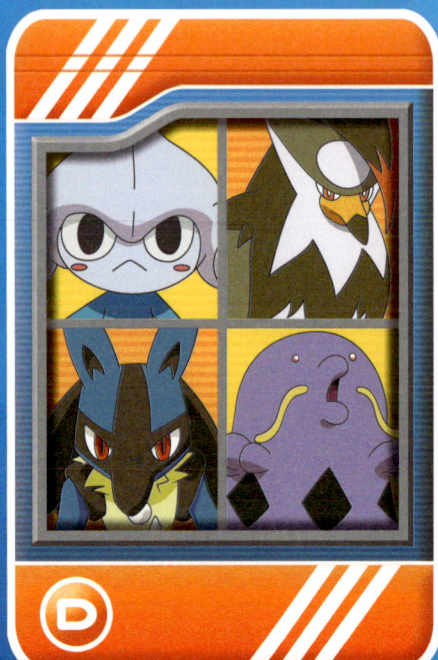

SINNOH SHUFFLE

TAKE A LOOK AT THIS LIST OF BIZARRE NAMES, MIX THEM UP AND YOU'LL DISCOVER SOME OF SINNOH'S FINEST POKÉMON. NOW MATCH THEM WITH THE CLOSE-UPS ON THE RIGHT.

1. ARIOCUL

2. RATSVIAA

3. BRAYNUE

4. TIDEEMIT

5. USCARHIPI

One of these Pokémon is not mentioned in either of the stories. Stick a picture of it here.

6. MACHIRCH

ANSWERS

Page 42 - Veilstone Values

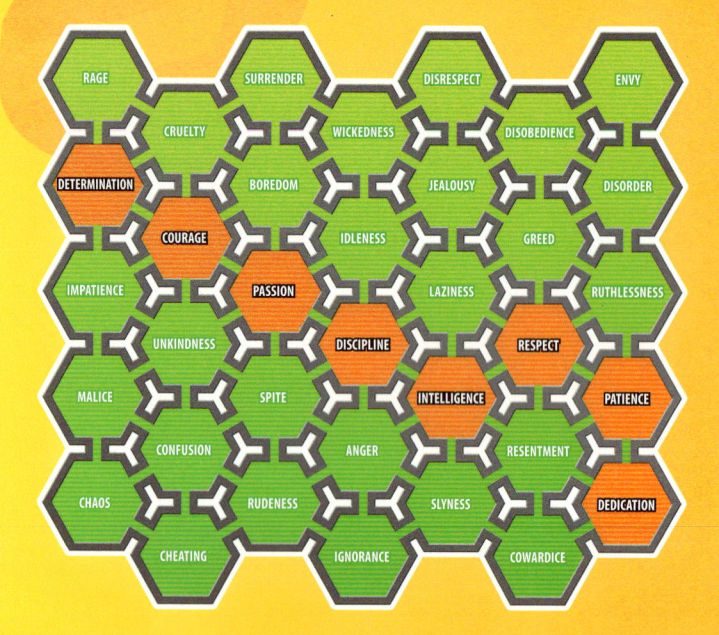

Page 45 - Fire and Ice Wordsearch

Page 44 - Maylene's Maze

Page 48 - Pick a Pokédex

SCREEN D

Page 49 - Sinnoh Shuffle

1. LUCARIO
2. STARAVIA
3. BUNEARY
4. MEDITITE
5. PACHIRISU
6. CHIMCHAR

PACHIRISU IS NOT MENTIONED IN THE STORIES.